NOAH
AND THE GREAT FLOOD

RETOLD AND ILLUSTRATED BY WARWICK HUTTON

A MARGARET K. McELDERRY BOOK

ATHENEUM   1977   NEW YORK

This book is for Han

Library of Congress Cataloging in Publication Data
Hutton, Warwick.
Noah and the great flood.
"A Margaret K. McElderry book."
SUMMARY: An interpretation of the familiar Bible story
using a simple text based on the King James version.
1. Deluge—Juvenile literature. 2. Noah—Juvenile literature.
3. Bible. O.T.—Biography—Juvenile literature. [1. Noah's ark. 2. Bible stories—O.T.] I. Title.
BS658.H87   222'.11'09505   77-3217
ISBN 0-689-50098-X

Published simultaneously in Canada by McClelland & Stewart, Ltd.
Manufactured in the United States of America
by Eastern Press, Inc., New Haven, Connecticut
Bound by A. Horowitz & Son/Bookbinders, Fairfield, New Jersey
First Edition

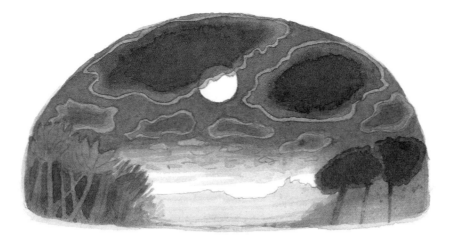

In the beginning, after the earth had been formed, men began to multiply and cover the land. There was great wickedness among them everywhere, and God was sorry to have created men who were so filled with violence. He decided to destroy both men and beasts from the face of the earth.

But Noah was a good man, and he found grace in the eyes of the Lord. He walked with God.

Noah had three sons. They were called Shem, Ham, and Japheth.

God said to Noah, "Because the earth is so filled with the evil of men, I will destroy them all. You must build an ark of gopher wood. It shall be three hundred cubits long, fifty cubits wide, and thirty high. It shall have three decks and a door in the side. You must cover it with pitch both inside and outside to keep it dry.

"Then I will bring a flood of water upon the earth so that everything will drown, both man and beast. But you and your family, together with a pair of each living thing—every bird and animal from the earth and the sky—I promise to save."

Noah did all God commanded and built the ark.

God said to Noah, "You must take all your household into the ark and two of every animal—each beast and bird and creeping thing—to keep their kind alive. You must take all the food to be eaten by yourselves and the wild animals. In seven days time I will make the rain come to destroy every living thing on the face of the earth."

Noah did all God had commanded him.

Seven days later the rain began, and Noah, who was six hundred years old at that time, went into the ark with the whole of his family—his wife, their sons and their sons' wives—and following him, two by two, came the animals he had collected.

Soon all the land and even the mountains were covered, and everything on its surface died—birds, cattle, beasts, and men. Only Noah remained alive and those that were with him.

Then the fountains of the great deep were released, and the windows of heaven were opened, and the waters increased, but the ark was borne up and floated above the land.

After forty days and nights, God made a wind pass over the earth, and the rain ceased.

Noah opened a window in the ark and sent forth a raven which flew to and fro until it disappeared.

Then he sent forth a dove, but she could find nowhere to land and she returned to Noah who put out his hand and took her back into the ark.

After waiting seven days he again sent forth the dove. In the evening of that day the dove returned with an olive leaf in her beak, so Noah knew the floods had begun to go down.

Seven days later he released the dove once more. She flew off and never returned.

The waters of the flood continued to go down, and after one hundred and fifty days the ark came to rest on the mountains of Ararat.

When the ground around the ark was dry, God said to Noah, "Come out of the ark, you and your family, and bring all the animals and birds, so that you may spread over the earth again and be fruitful and multiply."

So they all came out, back to dry land. The first thing Noah did was to make a sacrifice to God for preserving them all.

In return, God promised never to destroy the earth again,
however evil men became. God blessed Noah and told him to
multiply and increase throughout the earth and to rule over it.

Between heaven and earth He set a rainbow to show His
promise that He would never bring another flood to destroy
all earth's living things.

THE
END